IMAGES
of America

HOUSTON
POLICE DEPARTMENT

Mayor Kathy Whitmire took a bold historic step in April 1982 when she appointed Lee P. Brown Houston's police chief, the first African American to head a major city's police department. The first-term appointment proved to be the most significant in Houston police history. Brown diversified the department, enhanced education opportunities, and opened it up to minority and gay communities for the first time. In doing so, he changed the "us-versus-them" attitude that had previously prevailed in these areas. For the first time, Brown's Community-Oriented Policing provided community leaders with the opportunity to help determine the crime-fighting strategies in their neighborhoods. (Kathy Whitmire.)

ON THE COVER: Percy Heard, head of this Houston Police Department (HPD) Pistol Team, is clad in the light vested suit, second from the right, and was very likely the best pistol shooter in the bunch. One day, while returning from his lunch hour, the chief saw that a lone gunman was robbing a drugstore. He parked his car nearby, walked into the store, and shot the robber between the eyes. The pistol team members pictured are, from left to right, Buffalo Huddleston, Dan Blalock, unidentified, Percy Heard, and unidentified. Those not pictured are Little Mike Meinke and Big Mike Meinke. (Sloane Collection.)

IMAGES
of America

HOUSTON
POLICE DEPARTMENT

Tom Kennedy
Foreword by Lee Brown, PhD

ARCADIA
PUBLISHING

Published by Arcadia Publishing
Charleston, South Carolina

Printed in the United States of America

Library of Congress Control Number: 2011943059

For all general information, please contact Arcadia Publishing:
Telephone 843-853-2070
Fax 843-853-0044
E-mail sales@arcadiapublishing.com
For customer service and orders:
Toll-Free 1-888-313-2665

Visit us on the Internet at www.arcadiapublishing.com

To the men and women in HPD Blue—past, present, and future.

CONTENTS

FOREWORD

I had the privilege of serving as chief of the Houston Police Department from 1982 to 1990. During that time, it was my pleasure to work with numerous men and women who went into the streets every day doing the important work of protecting Houstonians.

In addition, I had the opportunity to meet or hear about many others who served prior to my arrival. I also had the opportunity to meet Tom Kennedy of the *Houston Post*, who always demonstrated himself as an accomplished journalist who thoroughly researched his articles to ensure accuracy. In this book, Tom has done an outstanding job telling the story of the Houston Police Department through pictures and brief narratives.

Starting with the time Houston was first developed by the Allen brothers in 1836 and the creation of the city's first police department in 1841, the reader is provided with a succinct, yet clear, understanding of the evolution of the HPD. Many of the photographs are rare and with the narratives provide the reader with an understanding of the department's transformation. It depicts a clear history with the ups and downs, the good and the bad.

The readers' interest is also captured by pictures of individuals who played key roles in HPD history. For example, the city's first chief of police, its first minority and female officers, the first minorities and females to be promoted, and so on. The book ends, and rightfully so, by paying tribute to the many brave men and women who made the ultimate sacrifice for their fellow citizens.

Telling the history of an organization through pictures is unique, yet this book is both educational and enjoyable. I am honored to have played a small role in the history of the Houston Police Department. It is a history that has been brilliantly told by this unique publication. I recommend it to anyone interested in the metamorphosis of the Houston Police Department, an institution so important to the life of the City of Houston.

Lee Brown, PhD
Chief of the Houston Police Department
1982–1990
Mayor of the City of Houston
1998–2004

ACKNOWLEDGMENTS

This book would not have been possible without the many individuals who helped me gather photographs to tell the story of the Houston Police Department, starting with founding HPD Museum director Denny Hair. Police Chief Charles McClelland enabled the launch with his administrative staff members Dennis Carter, Craig Ferrell, Jim Jones, Jessica Sloman, Regina Woolfolk, John Cannon, and Jeff Monk; talented HPD photographers Tim Palmer, Lance White, Matt Fowler, Larry Curley, and Jenna Whyte; and assistants Norma Utley and Dorothy Willegas.

Special thanks go to the following people: HPD Museum director James Chapman; Krystal LaReau and Daisy Gutierrez of the Houston Police Officers Union; HPOU presidents, past and present, Hans Marticiuc, Gary Blankinship, J.J. Berry, and Ray Hunt; HPOU executive director Mark Clark; former narc and police union pioneer Bob Thomas; and Sgt. Tom Hayes for help and encouragement. Thanks also to retired HPD Homicide Division lieutenant Nelson Zoch for his masterwork, *Fallen Heroes of the Bayou City*. I can't thank Mary Pyland enough for sharing her talents in this picture story and to her husband, Senior Police Officer Freddie Joe Pyland.

I thank Phil Archer of KPRC-TV; Rick Hartley of the 100 Club of Greater Houston; former reporter and police spokesman Fred King; and Joel Draut, Houston Metropolitan Research Center (HMRC) archivist and the *Houston Post*'s last chief photographer. I have special thanks to Shirley Cato, Sarah Canby Jackson of the Harris County Archives, Camp Logan collector Robbie Morin, the family of Mayor Louie Welch, and Welch's right-hand-man Homer Harris. I thank fellow Arcadia authors/friends Mike Vance, Ann Becker, and Story Sloane III as well as J.R. Gonzales of the *Houston Chronicle*. For technical assistance, I thank Rhonda Glassgow, Daniel Nugent, and Elsie Nguyen of Wolf Camera.

I couldn't have done this without my wife, Glenda (my greatest editor), son Chris and his wife Laura, and daughter Claire. Many thanks to them for technical help when I thought the software was foisting me into the Internet equivalent of the Gulf of Mexico. I also had a phenomenal editor, Lauren Hummer, who gets a gold star for understanding the ways of an old newspaper columnist.

INTRODUCTION

Houston began as a developer's town in 1836. Developers Augustus and John Allen of New York produced well-circulated advertisements touting their new development as "a most beautiful site for a town" with hills, spring water, pine timber for construction, and a navigable bayou for enterprising barge and steamboat businesses.

Like many successful American developers over the centuries, the Allen brothers also wisely gauged the political waters, naming their new development after Gen. Sam Houston, the hero of the Battle of San Jacinto, which won Texas its independence from Mexico. That battle was won in April 1836; the Allens formally established their new town in August. General Houston became the first president of the Republic of Texas, and the budding development bearing his name immediately became the capital.

Lots went up for sale at moderate terms. Prospective residents quartered themselves in small tents and drank, gambled, and socialized with others in larger ones. The first lodging with an actual roof was a small steamer, which had made the 10-hour trip from Galveston on the Gulf of Mexico to the south. The city of Houston incorporated on June 5, 1837. The sheriff was "the law."

There were laws against various kinds of gambling, which did not stop the plethora of green-felt tables and thoroughbred racing. When alleged criminals were caught and tried on the sheriff's watch, the punishments ranged from fines and jail terms to lashing, branding, or hanging. Most of the crimes resulted from too much whiskey, gambling disputes, or both.

In 1841, Houston, under its first mayor and two aldermen, established the city's police force by hiring two constables at $60 monthly salaries. The first city "jail" was actually city hall, with the police court on the upper story and the cell block on the first floor. Trials were informally conducted without necessarily following formal rules of evidence. The city marshal, subject to election to one-year terms, also collected taxes as part of his statutory duties, which paid $2,000 annually. From 1863 through 1868, Isaac C. Lord served as marshal and was the only marshal to later become mayor of Houston until Lee Brown in 1998. The mid-1800s began a tradition that lasted past World War II: the mayor picked out all of his police officers, basically making them political appointees.

The financially troubled years after the Civil War required officer layoffs and marked the first appearance of African Americans with badges. Lord established a code of conduct and bravely resisted the Union's military control by refusing to give way to an appointed marshal as a replacement. Lord lasted into the next year and became mayor in 1875 after the postwar military reign. His leadership helped to establish the force's first rules manual and to standardize the first-ever official police uniforms consisting of a navy-blue, indigo-dyed frock coat with short rolling collar that fastened at the neck and met "halfway between the articulation of the hip joint and the knee."

The number of African American officers never reached more than three before the turn of the century, when the Houston Police Force amounted to 25 to 30 officers, including the marshal (police chief). The job of mounted patrol officers consisted mainly of rounding up stray cattle and horses. The primary cause of crime was the growing number of saloons and gambling establishments.

It was difficult to keep track of the precise number of officers killed in the line of duty. C. Edward Foley was the first on record, suffering shotgun wounds on Market Square in the center of downtown. Foley's killer was nearly lynched on the spot. Officers Richard Snow, Henry Williams, and James E. Fenn died in the line of duty before 1900, the year that changed the title of the head of the department from marshal to police chief. John G. Blackburn was the last marshal, and his successor, George Ellis, was the first to hold the new title and, in doing so, became the last elected chief in history. Henceforth, the mayor would appoint the chief.

The year 1910 marked some major milestones in the Houston Police Department. J.M. Ray, a 19-year police veteran, faced new challenges head-on, making it clear what he wanted from each officer who protected the 78,880 residents of Texas's largest city. Traffic patrol officers on horses gave way to solo motorcycle officers to write speeding citations for the drivers of a growing number of automobiles.

The very first patrol car was placed into operation at a time when officers were paid $2.66 daily. Houses of prostitution were against the law but tolerated. On April 1, 1910, Deputy Chief William E. Murphy was shot and killed in a downtown café by a disgruntled former officer he had recently fired. The shooter was found not guilty, arguing self-defense. Murphy was the highest-ranking officer to have died in the line of duty.

Six different individuals served as chief between 1910 and 1913. Chief Ben Davison was the most highly respected leader of the lot but he was gone from the department by the time HPD experienced its bloodiest day in history, August 23, 1917. Five officers lost their lives in what would become known as the Camp Logan Riot. Soldiers in the predominately African American camp west of downtown felt victimized by the prevailing Jim Crow laws. Many of them grew angry with the report that a mounted officer had arrested a black soldier for allegedly interfering with the arrest of a black woman. False rumors ruled the day, the first being that the black officer involved was killed. Later, word on the street had it that a mob of white citizens was armed and approaching the camp. Subsequently, a black sergeant led 100 fellow soldiers toward downtown, killing 15 whites—including five officers—and wounding 12 others. Four black soldiers also died, including the leader, who committed suicide. The largest series of courts martial in American history were conducted as a result of the riot. In all, 118 soldiers faced charges; 110 of them were found guilty, and 19 were hanged.

During this period, civil service laws required by a 1914 charter change supposedly generated a route of appeal for dismissed officers seeking their jobs back. But the mayor controlled the appointees to both the commission and the department throughout the 1920s, 1930s, and 1940s, placing Houston in the ranks of cities with the most potent, strong mayoral forms of government in the nation. One's ability to be hired and to retain his job as an officer depended almost entirely on his political patronage.

HPD historian Denny Hair pointed out, "The integrity of the commission was further compromised by the right of the city council to veto or amend the rules proposed by the commission." Political appointment of officers caused mistrust by the citizenry and an almost constant air of job insecurity for officers who could be demoted from captain to patrol officer after an election. Local ordinances or civil service commission policies prohibited strikes, collective bargaining, unions, and, in most cases, the right to appeal firings for civil service violations.

HPD had one of the nation's most detailed police rules manuals, consisting of 92 pages and requiring officers to work 12-hour days. No officer could use tobacco or read a newspaper while on duty. Technically, the chief was called "the superintendent," a title that was seldom formally used until 1934. Four years later the title became "chief," used to this day to identify the department's chief executive.

The department, through the efforts of Chief Davison, gained nationwide attention with the establishment of a fingerprint system and the development of this innovative identification method to the highest point of efficiency. In 1918, Eva Jane Bacher became HPD's first female police officer. Previously, females on the force were known as matrons and had no arrest power. Bacher worked with the public morale and safety squad in 1920 before becoming the first female detective in 1921, as Houston's population reached 138,276.

The 1920s saw the entry of an individual who would have a strong influence over Houston policing on and off for the next four decades. Oscar F. Holcombe was elected mayor five times in the 1920s and three times in each of the following decades. Mayor Holcombe did a lot of hiring and firing of officers. One captain before one of Holcombe's elections was blowing a whistle at a downtown intersection as soon as Holcombe was sworn in for his next term.

Officers were virtual political pawns, who were often required to pass out campaign literature or knock on doors for the incumbent. In 1933, Holcombe administratively combined the police and fire departments and appointed his campaign manager, George Woods, as the public safety director. This practice lasted until a new mayor was elected in 1937. But for four years, two mayoral terms, Woods saw to it that Holcombe supporters were promoted—sometimes from sergeant to captain overnight.

The 1920s, 1930s, and 1940s saw many Houston policing firsts: first substation (Magnolia) in 1926, first car radio in 1927, first in-service police school in 1930, first police academy class in 1939, first operator hired to handle police service calls in 1940, and—in an action that changed the course of HPD history—the passage of the first civil service law that provided job protection for officers. The latter event took place in 1947 when Gov. Beauford H. Jester signed into law what became known as Article 1269m of Texas civil service law.

The new law was made possible by resourceful leaders on the force who met in secret planning sessions while in fear of losing their jobs. They took the bold steps needed to gain the support of sympathetic members of the Texas legislature. This came in an era when rural senators and state representatives appreciated the importance of brave men who needed job protection to support their families.

The passage of 1269m firmly established the Houston Police Officers Association. Consisting of a vast majority of the officers on the force, the association studied the city budget and issued well-studied plans for annual pay raises that also affected firefighters and civilian employees. Association leaders, buoyed by the legislative success of 1269m, continued to strengthen their relationships with both Houston councilmen and state legislators. That practice grew into a potent political action committee that remains effective to this day.

The 1952 opening of the new headquarters at 61 Riesner Street also provided an adjacent police academy to train cadets. The first academy class of the modern era was graduated in 1948, nine years since the class of 1939. No cadet classes were held during World War II. Crime levels after the war necessitated the training of more officers, many of whom were war veterans returning to their hometown, nicknamed "the Bayou City."

Walkie-talkies, civilian jailers, the first professionally trained polygraph operator, and the demand for a state-of-the-art facility that became known as the Crime Lab marked the major changes in the HPD of the 1950s. Under police chief Jack Heard, the son of Houston police chief Percy Heard, the police academy opened to women for the first time in 1955. Jack Heard was the first and only sergeant to be promoted directly to chief, a promotion that literally doubled his salary. He instituted the first lightweight cotton uniform shirts, the first helmets for motorcycle officers, and abolished the shoulder straps on the traditional Sam Browne belts. Heard also was the first chief to wear a uniform to work every day and the first to appoint a full-time chaplain.

Like many other departments in the postwar policing era, HPD endured its share of bad apples in the barrel. Prewar police chief Ray Ashworth, the second outsider to serve in the position, having come from San Antonio, actually learned in 1941 that 15 officers had prior criminal records and tried unsuccessfully to fire them. Ashworth reorganized the department and was a stickler for his rules and policies, including one-man patrol cars and loudspeakers on squad cars to call attention to traffic safety issues. The requirements reflected his belief in high-tech training and more education requirements, a path also followed later on by Heard and his predecessor, Chief L.D. Morrison Sr., for whom the new police academy, opened in 1981, was named.

Before Ashworth left for wartime Army service, he made it clear that the department fit three descriptions it would experience throughout modern history: undermanned, under-equipped, and underfunded. His replacement was Percy Heard, Jack's father and HPD's chief in both the Depression and World War II. It became Percy Heard's job to oversee the Houston Auxiliary Police Force, consisting of "trained" civilians who carried badges and guns. Initially, their primary job was to keep the city safe from saboteurs. This part of the force grew to more than 300 men.

The department experienced the leadership of six chiefs under four mayors between the war years and 1964. As in the 1930s, the mayor's chair at city hall was occupied mostly by Oscar Holcombe, who also served from 1947 through 1953 and for a final term in 1956 and 1957. But the man known as "the Gray Fox" had to use a different modus operandi because of the civil service laws protecting officers. Following Holcombe, a major turning point in HPD history happened when Mayor Louie Welch (1964–1974) selected Herman Short to be his police chief.

Short (1964–1973) served longer than any other chief in Houston history. The tough-minded chief's tough rule enforcement and fairness kept morale at a generally high level. Like many departments in the United States, HPD was gradually transitioning into a more diverse operation, which experienced often-dramatic events connected to the civil rights movement and the anti–Vietnam War era.

Short was not known to recruit minorities or women and had a low tolerance for civil disobedience. Yet the leadership exuded by Welch and Short effectively curbed several brief incidents of violence. The Bayou City's only brush with rioting came in 1967 at the predominately African American Texas Southern University when one white police officer was killed in gunfire exchanged between officers and students. It was the only violent outbreak in which more whites than blacks were killed: one white and no blacks.

The Welch-Short years gave way to transition from a city still embedded in the outmoded Jim Crow laws to leadership at both city hall and HPD, which saw a sharp increase in minority recruiting. In the 1970s, the department went through events involving a Hispanic individual who drowned in Buffalo Bayou while in police custody as well as several others involving the deaths of young white men in custody.

There came another turning point in April 1982 when reform-minded Mayor Kathy Whitmire appointed Lee P. Brown as chief. Brown was the first African American to head a police department in a major American city. He served more than seven years before becoming New York's police commissioner, Pres. Bill Clinton's drug czar, and Houston's mayor for six years.

Brown vowed to lead the police department to serve every community in Houston, from the mostly gay neighborhoods to those that housed blacks, Hispanics, and the ever-growing Asian population. He pioneered Community-Oriented Policing, a concept requiring officers to work directly with neighborhood leaders to fight the specific criminal elements in their areas. Many Houston historians believe Brown's appointment was the most important one in HPD history because he helped diversify its makeup and initiated community-policing partnerships that changed the previous "us-versus-them" attitudes in minority communities. As mayor, he opened the door to the Houston Police Officers Union (previously known as the association) to establish a meet-and-confer process that led to better pay and other benefits.

By 2011, the department had become the most diversified and well educated in history. Brown was followed by the city's first female police chief, Elizabeth "Betsy" Watson, and four other individuals, including three other African American chiefs. HPD became better equipped but was still considered to be undermanned at 5,400 officers and always underfunded. About two out of every five officers are people of color, and more than half have at least one college degree.

One

THE EARLY YEARS

Sam Houston, the hero of the Battle of San Jacinto and the first president of the Republic of Texas, established a company of Texas Rangers as part of his earliest duties. This is a picture of an early Texas Ranger. The initial duties of this individual had nothing to do with keeping the peace on the streets of the city named for the great hero. The Texas Rangers' function was to fight Indians. That later changed, of course. (HPD Museum.)

The Allen brothers, who developed Houston beginning in 1836, sent this artist's rendering of their new city in flyer format to prospective new residents from other states. They took liberties with the new city's real topography. The low-lying Bayou City has no hills to this day, except for the manmade versions known as freeways. (HPD Museum.)

Officer William A. Weiss was on nighttime patrol of downtown when a drunk having a bad day shot him four times during a brief argument on July 30, 1901. Weiss was the fifth known Houston police officer to die in the line of duty and the first in the new century. (Nelson Zoch.)

On December 11, 1901, 18-year veteran officer Herman Youngst (right) responded to Det. John C. James (below), who had just been shot by known gambler Sid Preacher. Youngst was shot in the back and killed after fighting with Preacher, who was able to once again use his double-barrel shotgun. Preacher then used the butt of his gun to make sure Youngst was dead. Within seconds, the severely wounded James used his pistol to shoot Preacher three or four times, killing him before he died. (Nelson Zoch.)

Here, an unidentified defendant's neck is being placed inside the noose at a location somewhere near downtown Houston in 1880. The earliest punishments for convicted criminals were lashing, branding, being sentenced to prison—or hanging. (HPD Museum.)

This early photograph from the 1870s shows that Houston had some hustle and bustle, which, unfortunately, drew more illegal acts and required policemen to patrol the streets day and night. (HPD Museum.)

Pictured is the prime downtown patrol area for the Houston Police Department in the 1880s. (HPD Museum.)

Isaac Lord served as the elected town marshal from 1863 to 1868. Lord was the first of only two individuals who first headed the police department and later became mayor of Houston. Lord earned $2,000 annually and was the first to establish rules that governed the conduct of the police force. (HPD Museum.)

This was the first "modern" Houston police station in 1894. The first city "jail" was actually part of city hall and police court. (HPD Museum.)

This silver badge No. 5 is the oldest badge in the Houston Police Museum collection. The shield is still used today in an updated version. (HPD Museum.)

The first HPD detective badge was round and flat. (HPD Museum.)

John G. Blackburn was the last head of HPD (1898–1902) who went by the title of marshal. His successor George Ellis was the first individual designated as "police chief" and the last to be popularly elected. (HPD Museum.)

J.M. Ray succeeded George Ellis as police chief and served about one year. That brief tenure did not stop him from designing one of the fanciest badges in HPD history. (HPD Museum.)

Ray's badge featured a large diamond in the center. (HPD Museum.)

Two

TURN OF THE CENTURY

This is probably one of the most famous photographs in HPD history. It depicts the department in about 1909. The moustachioed gentleman in the black hat in the center of the first row is Deputy Chief William E. Murphy, the highest-ranking officer to die in the line of duty. He was shot to death on April 1, 1910, by ex-officer Earl McFarland, the frowning man also with a moustache, who is standing over Murphy's right shoulder. Murphy had fired McFarland, who still held a grudge. Although caught with "the smoking gun," McFarland claimed self defense, and a Galveston jury set him free. The man sitting to Murphy's left in the wide-brimmed hat is Chief George Ellis, the last elected chief in HPD history. (HPD Museum.)

Taken in 1915, this first picture of every division in HPD tells the story of a turn-of-the century policing agency in a fast-growing city in the South. (HPD Museum.)

These HPD mounted patrol officers are depicted with two early canine officers with their police dogs in 1915. (HPD Museum.)

The second HPD station at 401 Caroline Street actually served as both a police and fire station, beginning in 1923. This early panorama of the department in the 1920s was taken in front of the station. (HMRC.)

The first traffic tower in downtown Houston was designed to provide officers the ability to direct traffic from the safety of a tower instead of at ground level. HPD quit the practice when an errant vehicle knocked over the tower for the last time. Fortunately, no one was seriously injured. (HMRC.)

Eva Jane Bacher, the only woman in this picture, was the department's first female detective. In 1917, she graduated from matron status to a badge-carrying officer because of the growing number of wayward girls and a greater need for social services, especially in downtown. When a new chief took office, he did not like the idea of a policewoman and fired Bacher under a policy that enabled him to do so "for the good of the service." (HPD Museum.)

This is probably the earliest photograph, taken in 1910, of HPD mounted patrol officers. Note the shield badges, which became standard for HPD. (HPD Museum.)

By 1910, all Houston officers were required to report over the Gamewell boxes every hour. Gamewells were call boxes established on most every street corner downtown. A patrol was sent to locations where the beat officer failed to report. HPD was one of 44 departments in the United States that put the call boxes to immediate use. (HPD Museum.)

Troops gather in formation along the primary "street" through Camp Logan. The worst riot in Houston's history happened when an Army unit consisting of African Americans from Northern states was assigned to guard Camp Logan as it was being constructed at the site of the current Memorial Park. The attitude of a growing city with Southern traditions and Jim Crow laws in effect soon developed bad feelings between the black soldiers and white citizens, including the police. (Robbie Morin Collection.)

A black military policeman took exception to the arrest of a partially drunk black solider and a Fourth Ward resident, resulting in his own arrest. False rumors ruled the day, which went down as the bloodiest in HPD history on August 23, 1917. This is an overall view of the camp, which had very few permanent wooden structures at the time. (Robbie Morin Collection.)

Troops gather for rifle inspection at Camp Logan. The first rumor was that officers killed the meddling soldier. The second rumor was that a white mob was on its way to deal with this soldier's buddies. More than 100 black soldiers armed themselves and tore off toward downtown. They killed 15 whites—including five HPD officers—and wounded 12 others. The violent outbreak also resulted in the deaths of five soldiers and the largest series of courts martial in US military history. In all, 110 black soldiers were found guilty, and 19 were hanged. (Robbie Morin Collection.)

Of the five HPD officers killed, historians have recovered pictures of only three. The five who gave their lives protecting Houstonians that violent day were officers Rufus H. Daniels, Edwin G. Minecke, Horace Moody, Ross Patton, and Ira D. Raney. (Nelson Zoch.)

Pictured here is Horace Moody, one of the five HPD officers killed. (Nelson Zoch.)

27

Pictured here is Ira C. Raney, another one of the five HPD officers killed. (Nelson Zoch.)

A solo motorcycle officer appears to be writing a ticket to the driver of a 1929 model Stutz in downtown Houston. (Sloane Collection.)

The 1928 Democratic National Convention nominated Al Smith for president. The city of Houston built a wooden structure, Sam Houston Hall, for the event. It practically abutted the downtown fire station No. 2. Depicted here are the firefighters on the right and two Houston police officers at the gate of the hall. (Sloane Collection.)

Two of Houston's finest are posed outside the location of Sam Houston, which gave way to the Sam Houston Coliseum and Music Hall complex in 1937, located in the next block away from city hall. (Sloane Collection.)

This is the Houston Police baseball team in the 1930s. (HPD Museum.)

This c. 1930 photograph of Houston homicide detectives highlighted the "hat tradition" of their lot throughout HPD history up until the late 1960s. (HPD Museum.)

Hermann Square became a public park in 1914, about 25 years before city hall was built on the western edge. The square was lined with huge live oak trees with landscaping provided around a reflecting basin. City benefactor George Hermann once permitted his laborers to sleep off their hangovers in this block, which he believed was cheaper than bailing them all out of jail. When Hermann donated the land for a park, he insisted on a provision permitting people to sleep in the park. Then and now, HPD officers do not prohibit sleeping in this park for fear of violating Hermann's terms. (Sloane Collection.)

Houston City Hall was constructed in 1938 and adjoins Hermann Square. It looks essentially the same today with more elaborate landscaping and some architectural updates. This photograph was taken in the 1960s. (HPD Archives.)

Percy Heard, head of this HPD Pistol Team, is the man in the middle and was very likely the best pistol shooter in the bunch. One day, while returning from his lunch hour, the chief saw that a lone gunman was robbing a drugstore. He parked his car nearby, walked into the store, and shot the robber between the eyes. The pistol team members are, from left to right, Buffalo Huddleston, Dan Blalock, unidentified, Percy Heard, unidentified, Little Mike Meinke, and Big Mike Meinke. (Sloane Collection.)

Detectives wore the round badge in the early part of the 20th century. This badge No. 2 is from 1915. (HPD Museum.)

This panorama of HPD was taken in Hermann Park on November 10, 1931, when the department was under the direction of Chief Percy Heard. Note the segregated African American officers off to the right. (HMRC.)

Police Chief Percy Heard served as Houston's chief both in the Depression and during World War II. Chief Heard was highly respected by his officers, elected officials at City Hall, and his fellow Houstonians. His son Jack was later chief, the only father-son police chiefs in history. (HPPU Archives.)

Officers began wearing star badges in 1915, but the department soon went back to the traditional shield design, which is still in use today. (HPD Museum.)

Three

HPD IN TRAINING

Here is HPD's first-ever academy-trained class from 1939, known as the "real" class No. 1, even though the 1948 class carries the official designation. Mayor Oscar Holcombe (white suit) is pictured with the class. Capt. L.D. Morrison Sr. is on the far left, with Chief Lawrence C. Brown between him and the mayor. Morrison is known as the father of HPD academic training, and the present-day police academy carries his name. (HPPU Archives.)

With their eyes right, HPD cadets from the late 1950s to early 1960s are under the stern watch of their sergeant. (HPD Archives.)

Six cadets from academy class No. 18 pose in 1954 with their instructors Sgt. Richard Lineberger and Capt. Harry Caldwell. From left to right are G.V. Rodriguez, J.T. Gallemore, R.L. Lineberger, H.D. Caldwell, B.J. Fry, and G.L. Attebery. The two officers behind Fry and Attebery are unidentified. Caldwell later became police chief. (HPD Museum.)

Harry Caldwell was a Marine drill instructor before he joined HPD. Here, he is seen in a classroom setting at the Houston Police Academy at 61 Riesner Street in 1956. (HPD Museum.)

Cadet class No. 16 in 1957 included officer Al Blair, far left, one of two African Americans in the class. The other was Fred Black. Blair served for 47 years and Black for 30. (HPD Museum.)

In the early years of the academy, cadets were trained to measure the length of skid marks to determine the speed of vehicles involved in collisions. (HPD Museum.)

These cadets undergo firearms training in the 1950s. (HPD Museum.)

Here, HPD cadets line up in 1963. (HPD Archives.)

This picture of five cadets from class No. 32 in 1966 was featured in a class yearbook/brochure. The cadets are, from left to right, Dennis Storemski, John Thornton, Mary Francis Stevens, Tom Tureck, and E. Urbani. (HPD Museum.)

Chief Jack Heard allowed the first four women to attend Houston Police Academy. Here, Heard is pictured with those first four graduates, from left to right, Addie Jean Smith, Jo Bankston, Mercedes Halvorsen Singleton, and Emily Rimmer Vasquez. (Jo Bankston.)

Of the first four female Houston Police Academy graduates, officer Jo Bankston served long enough to earn retirement. She married fellow officer J.C. Bankston. (Jo Bankston.)

Dennis Storemski, a graduating cadet in 1966, was the first Houston police officer to serve in every rank from officer to executive assistant chief. Considered for police chief by several Houston mayors, Storemski retired to head Houston's Office of Public Safety and Homeland Security. (Dennis Storemski.)

When the police academy was located at the downtown police station, the shooting range was under a nearby bridge over Buffalo Bayou. The somewhat muffled shots were well within earshot of passing motorists on their way to and from downtown, which was only a block away. (HPD Museum.)

The earliest HPD recruits from the 1950s wore "cadet" badges until graduation. They were also known as police trainee badges. Here, from the HPD Museum, is police trainee badge No. 930. (HPD Museum.)

The HPD under a series of chiefs appointed by Mayor Fred Hofheinz recruited more women and minorities than ever before. This is a picture of class No. 67. The third man from the left is police chief Carrol Lynn. (May Walker.)

Four

WHEELS, HOOVES, AND BLADES

J.M. Ray was chief when HPD got its first patrol car. Patrol calls were beginning to take too long for horses and even motorcycles. Ray himself frequently used the car. (HPD Museum.)

The HPD Mounted Patrol was discontinued during the wartime years of the 1940s but revived in 1983, thanks largely to Houston City Councilwoman Eleanor Tinsley, who gained a reputation for taking on any crusade she felt would contribute positively to Houston. When re-organized with 14 horses, the HPD Mounted Patrol covered downtown events. Over the more than a quarter of a century since, it has grown to 40 horses covering not only downtown but Memorial and Hermann Parks, while being utilized in crowd management, searches, parades, dignitary protection, and other appropriate special events. It ranks as the second largest unit of its kind in the nation. In December 2003, the HPD command was convinced by experts' demonstrations that metal shoes caused many injuries and behavioral problems with horses. Today, all HPD horses patrol barefoot. (HPD Museum.)

This was the state-of-the-art HPD Ford paddy wagon in the late 1940s. (HPPU Archives.)

HPD used this
paddy wagon
in 1964 or
thereabouts.
(HPD Archives.)

This new mobile crime lab vehicle emerged on the HPD front in the early 1950s. HPD personnel are, from left to right, police chemist Floyd McDonald, Lt. Breckenridge Porter, police identification examiner K.D. Swatzel, Det. George Chapman, and identification supervisor R.O. Queen. (Nelson Zoch.)

This is a typical HPD radio patrol car of the 1950s. (HPD Archives.)

Here, a new shift goes on duty at 61 Riesner Street with officers manning their 1957 Chrysler patrol cars. (HPD Archives.)

On occasion, special units like the three-wheeler motorcycles would muster into formations in Memorial Park. This picture from May 14, 1959, was used in an HPD annual report. (HPD Archives.)

This HPD three-wheel motorcycle is on patrol in downtown Houston in the mid-1950s. (HPD Archives.)

HPD got this new fleet of three-wheeler motorcycles in 1963. (HPD Archives.)

This 1952 HPD patrol car was restored for display in the Houston Police Museum. Founding museum director Denny Hair was an HPD officer throughout his tenure. Taken in the shadows of the modern Houston skyline, this photograph shows Hair in a vintage 1950s uniform. (HPD Museum.)

HPD officers pose with a "Houston-blue" patrol car from the 1960–1961 era below the skyline of Houston, prior to the Bayou City becoming "Space City." (HPD Museum.)

Here are more Chryslers! This is yet another fleet of new Chrysler squad cars in formation in front of 61 Riesner Street in 1961. (HPD Archives.)

Here, the new 1971 patrol car fleet has arrived in Houston but the cars are not yet outfitted with the standard equipment necessary to answer calls. (*Houston Post* photograph by Ray Covey; courtesy of HMRC.)

An early HPD recruiting van is shown here in the late 1970s or early 1980s. Note that the lettering on the side is in both English and Spanish to facilitate recruiting efforts in Houston's growing number of Hispanic communities. Police chiefs Pappy Bond and Harry Caldwell stepped up HPD's Hispanic recruitment. (HPD Archives.)

A rare car, this 1975 Gremlin experimental police vehicle failed to result in a fleet of HPD Gremlins. (HPD Archives.)

Louie Welch was mayor in 1970 when HPD got its first helicopters. Councilman Johnny Goyen (left) and police chief Herman Short (second from left) look on as Mayor Welch pins the "wings" on HPD's first helicopter crew. (Photograph by Homer Harris; courtesy of Louie Welch family.)

Mayor Welch was given the first official spin around the city in HPD's first helicopter. Various studies have reported that the visual range of police helicopter aircrews is 15 to 30 times the visual range of ground-based officers. (Photograph by Homer Harris; courtesy of Louie Welch family.)

This HPD helicopter made an emergency landing on a street in a neighborhood in 1978. No one was injured. (Ken DeFoor.)

FOX is seen over Houston. This HPD helicopter is on patrol near downtown Houston in 1978. The name FOX comes from the unit's registration identification, which is the letter "F." (HPD Archives.)

The 100 Club's Dave Morris presents the keys to the new SWAT hostage negotiation van to HPD in 1981. The officials present include 100 Club executive director Mary Cooper and club officer Bob Herrin on the far left. Morris (dark suit) is presenting the keys to Police Chief B.K. Johnson (light suit) as SWAT lieutenant Jim "Peter" Gunn stands between them. Next to Johnson are John Rader (second from right) and George Bolin (right), two longtime 100 Club stalwarts. (100 Club.)

The hostage negotiation van was the first of many special policing vehicles the 100 Club purchased for the Houston Police Department. It was metal-plated and could withstand many bullets. (100 Club.)

The 100 Club of Greater Houston presented this armored vehicle, christened "the Big Mamou," in 1987. The cost was $295,000. (100 Club.)

In the mid-1980s, HPD had its own robot. Sgt. J.C. Mosier, the chief public information officer at the time, demonstrates it here. Mosier also gained ever-lasting fame when, as a member of the HPD softball team, he pitched the only known slow-pitch no-hitter in police-league history. (J.C. Mosier.)

HPD officer Adrian Garcia demonstrates Mac the Robot to a group of Houston elementary school students. Garcia retired from HPD to serve three terms as a Houston City Council member before he was elected Harris County sheriff in 2008. (HPD Archives.)

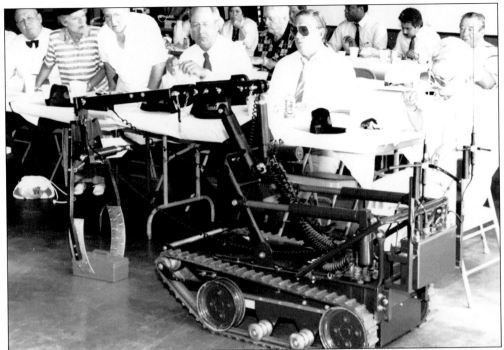

Unnamed and believed to be meaner than Mac, the bomb squad robot, another gift from the 100 Club of Greater Houston, was designed to undertake a lot more dangerous work. It was the first of its kind in the 1990s. Officials from the 100 Club on hand for the presentation were, from left to right, Jesse Charman, unidentified, John Rader, George Bolin, Nick Morrow (second row behind Bolin), Morton Cohn, and 100 Club executive director Mary Cooper. (100 Club.)

Bike officers head for duty in the 1990s. (HPD Archives.)

In the 1990s, this HPD Bicycle Patrol Unit was community sponsored and funded. The bike patrol officers proactively patrolled high-crime areas and pedalled through random residential and business neighborhoods. (HPD Archives.)

HPD's first mounted patrol was eliminated in the 1930s but re-emerged in 1984 as part of HPD Special Operations. Officer Gregory Sokoloski, left, ranked in 2012 as the senior member of mounted patrol. Sokoloski trained police officers in Poland in the use of horses. He is pictured here with Gen. Wojciech Olbrys, head of the Polish police delegation, which learned crowd control in Houston in March 2010. Magdalena Denham, right, served as interpreter. (Tom Kennedy.)

HPD's Mounted Patrol is the second largest unit of its kind in the United States, ranking behind only New York City. Here, the unit is participating in a crowd control drill in March 2010. (Tom Kennedy.)

In this photograph, HPD's Mounted Patrol demonstrates the use of police officers and their horses in the protection of a visiting dignitary. This was a drill used in the presence of visiting officers from Poland, who were in Houston to learn crowd control in preparation for Poland's 2012 World Cup Soccer Championship. (Tom Kennedy.)

Five

ON DUTY

This is headquarters! In the 1940s, Riesner Street and Houston Avenue was one of Houston's busiest intersections. In the early 1950s, HPD opened its new headquarters nearby. This photograph was taken in the 1960s. (HPD Archives.)

Here is the police headquarters at 61 Riesner Street shortly after it opened in the 1950s. (HPD Archives.)

Taken in January 1960, this photograph is looking east toward downtown via Allen Parkway, the major route to exclusive River Oaks. (HPD Archives.)

The Houston Story was a police mystery movie filmed in Houston, starring Gene Berry, Barbara Hale, and Edward Arnold. The city's new police station was shown in the film. (Tom Kennedy's Collectibles.)

Patrol officers from the HPD interview a witness in an inner-city neighborhood in the late 1950s. (HPD Archives.)

This photograph captures a typical day at HPD's garage in the mid-1950s. (HPD Archives.)

HPD's gym at 61 Riesner Street was the scene of cadet drills as well as off-duty basketball games. (HPD Archives.)

This is where officers from 1952 "ran it through R and I," as in the Records and Identification division. (HPD Archives.)

Here is an HPD jailer from the 1950s when police headquarters had its own jail. (HPD Archives.)

HPD's polygraph operated in this fashion in the late 1950s. Jack Heard, the only HPD sergeant in history to be directly promoted to chief, was the department's first-ever polygraph operator. This is one of his successors posing with a "suspect." (HPD Archives.)

HPD's dispatch area was located on the top floor of 61 Riesner Street in the 1950s. (HPD Archives.)

HPD's modern crime lab proved to be problematic for the department at the beginning of the new century. This is a scene from 1952 when crime labs were just coming into their own as investigative tools for police. (HPD Archives.)

The Houston Homicide Division traditionally has become the permanent assignment to numerous officers, detectives, and sergeants over many decades. Pictured here are some of the old veterans. They are, from left to right, Sgts. E.T. "Gene" Yanchak, James H. "Jim" Binford, and Wayne Wendel; Lt. Breckenridge Porter; Lt. Nelson Zoch; and Capt. Richard Holland. Holland was captain over the homicide division when this picture was taken. Binford was in homicide long enough to handle what is believed to be more homicides than any Houston officer in history. (Nelson Zoch.)

Standing from left to right, homicide detectives Chester Massey and L.D. Morrison Jr., along with Capt. Weldon Waycott and Det. H.W. "Trigger" Rodgers have just arrested murder suspect William Cummings in 1954. (Nelson Zoch.)

Det. W.G. Eickenhorst is covering the scene of a slaying on Washington Avenue west of downtown in the 1960s. (*Houston Post* photograph by Fred Bunch; courtesy of W.G. Eickenhorst.)

In the late 1970s, HPD used huge air bags to upright overturned 18-wheelers. Houston's elaborate freeway system seems to average at least one overturned 18-wheeler a day. (W.G. Eickenhorst.)

Officer H.M. "Stockey" Gray (left), officer E.J. "String" Stringfellow (center), and officer G.D. Shelton display a large marijuana plant they confiscated in 1959. Gray and Stringfellow were the first African American narcotics officers on the force. (May Walker.)

Probably the most gruesome murder scene of the modern era emerged on a quiet neighborhood street in the Montrose section of Houston in 1965. Fred and Edwina Rogers were murdered, dismembered, and neatly placed inside the refrigerator. Responding to a call, officers C.A. Bullock and L.M. Barta approached the modest brick home. Bullock was the first to open the icebox and discover the grisly remains. (*Houston Post* photograph by Bill Goodwin; courtesy of HMRC.)

Patrol officer L.M. Barta (left), C.A. Bullock (center), and an unidentified officer are pictured outside the Rogers house during the initial investigation of the "Icebox Murders." (*Houston Post* photograph by Bill Goodwin; courtesy of HMRC.)

Charles Rogers, the son of Fred and Edwina Rogers, was a brilliant, reclusive geologist who had a pilot's license. Rogers served in the Navy in World War II. He is likely the only murder suspect in HPD history whose case remained open even after he was legally declared dead in a civil court in 1975. Two books of fiction were written about him, and some Kennedy conspiracy buffs believe Rogers was involved on the grassy knoll, although there has never been substantial proof of any kind. (HMRC.)

Homicide detective James P. Paulk inspects the icebox after the remains of Mr. and Mrs. Rogers were removed. (*Houston Post* photograph by Bill Goodwin; courtesy of HMRC.)

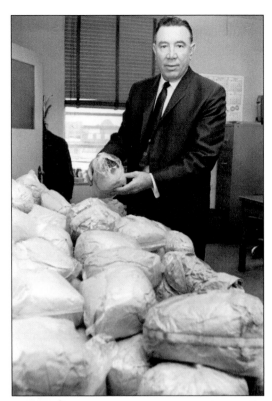

Longtime narcotics captain Jack Renois is photographed with more than 100 pounds of confiscated marijuana. The photograph was taken March 18, 1968. (*Houston Post* photograph; courtesy of HMRC)

These are the hands of a determined killer from the 1970s. The suspect was a paraplegic with limited use of his hands. He learned that his wife was running around on him, so he had a friend rig a loaded pistol in a specially designed hole in his lap tray and firmly tie a shoe string around the trigger, which he pulled with his teeth. (J.C. Mosier.)

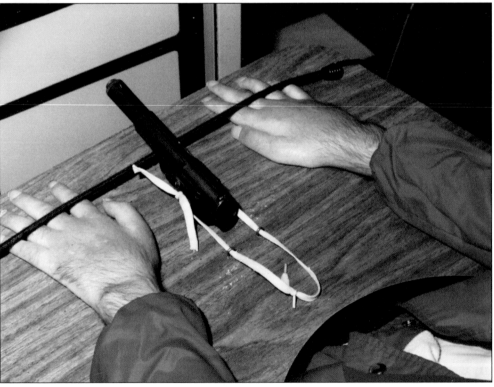

Homicide detective Johnny Bonds, left, poses with the capital murder suspect he had just arrested, Markham Duff-Smith. Bonds would not quit his investigation when a medical examiner ruled the death of a River Oaks couple and their 14-month-old son a double-murder/ suicide even though there was no murder weapon at the scene. Bonds spent two years proving the case was murder for hire in which four men were ultimately charged. The scheme to collect insurance was the brainchild of Duff-Smith, who was executed for his role. The case displayed one of the most determined investigations in HPD history. (Dan McAulty.)

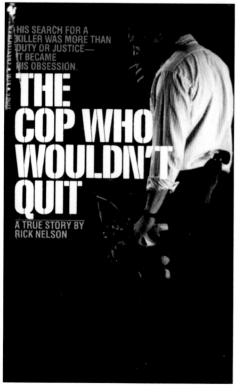

The Cop Who Wouldn't Quit, written by Houston Post reporter Rick Nelson in 1984, details Johnny Bonds's unyielding determination to prove an alleged murder/suicide was actually a murder for hire. And he did. (Johnny Bonds.)

Riot-helmeted HPD officers react to a violent demonstration in 1979 aimed at the Shah of Iran. (Ken DeFoor.)

HPD's Special Weapons and Tactics team was formed in 1974 and has an exciting and colorful history. SWAT is now better equipped to deal with terrorists, taking the lead to provide every Houston officer with active shooter training. SWAT's headquarters is a short drive from the heart of downtown Houston. This photograph was taken in 2009. Pictured are, from left to right, (first row) Ed Kwan, Richard Kent, Ed Lem, Manny Pierson, Steve Hamala, Mark Scales, Tony Pisaro, Julian Coleman, Glen Gold, Scott Warren, Ed Medrano, and Sgt. Bill Tweedie; (second row) Pat Straker, Justin Barber, D. Moreno, J. Zakharia, Hugo Gutierrez, Mike Carroll, Meredith Campbell, Travis Merrill, Gary Heath, Kevin Arntz, Lawrence Mouton, Thomas Hardin, Reynaldo Delasbour and Joe Hughes; (third row) Eric Holland, Marco Lopez, Sgt. J. Hudkins, Don Maulfair, Rich McCusker, Emory Desilites, Joel Salazar, Chris Stevens, Andy Orozco, Sgt. Tom Calabro, Lt. Albert Mihalco, Capt David Gott, Lt. Richard Besselman, Sgt. Dennis Garrett, Sgt. Chris Phillips, John Murphy, Steve Zakharia, Kyle Drey, Troy Dupuy, and George Griger. (SWAT.)

Here, SWAT members go through a drill near downtown. From left to right are Sandy Wall, Patrick Straker, Lawrence Mouton, and Gary Heath. (SWAT.)

Here SWAT is practicing a high-rise repelling drill. (HPD Archives.)

SWAT is pictured going through a drill near downtown. From left to right are Pat Straker, Sandy Wall, Ronnie Parker, and John Murphy. (HPD Museum.)

Technician N.L. LeBlanc examines some prints in his office inside the HPD latent lab on November 24, 1982. (HPD Archives.)

Chester Massey and Basil "Stu" Baker were wearing the hats that almost always identified homicide detectives in 1954 when the two worked an extra job at the Houston Livestock Show and Rodeo. Massey was a legend in the HPD, and Baker later became the US marshal for the Southern District of Texas. (HPD Archives.)

This scene from dispatch shows the initial step of a report from phase one to the next link in the chain needed to get it to patrol or the right investigative division. (HPD Archives.)

The chapel at the old City Prison Farm (P-Farm) was constructed in 1959. (HPD Archives.)

Here is the first group of people a suspect saw as he or she entered the booking office at the city jail in 1959. (HPD Archives.)

Male and female prisoners in the city jail were obviously separate. These archival photographs from September 20, 1977, depict the operations in the female section. (HPD Archives.)

This K-9 officer is preparing to demonstrate the skills of expertly trained police dogs to these boys and girls on a field trip to HPD. (HPD Archives.)

Chief Herman Short, center, poses at the graduation of the HPD Bomb Squad on February 26, 1965. Note that Short's picture is on the wall behind the group. (HPD Archives.)

Realizing the need for a full-time psychological counseling service, Police Chief Harry Caldwell chose Dr. Greg Riede as HPD's first counselor. Dr. Riede worked virtually 24 hours a day, seven days a week, and was described as a God-send by numerous officers. (Psych Services photograph.)

In 2012, Dr. Riede retired, and HPD was served with a full team of counselors, headed by Dr. Verdi R. Lethermon. The members of the psych services team are, from left to right, (first row) Maren F. Jones, PhD; Verdi R. Lethermon, PhD; and Dora Solorzano; (second row) Stephen. L. Tate, PsyD; Lisa Berg Garmezy, PhD; William E. Metcalfe, PhD; Benaye Boone; and George M. Wawrykow, PhD. (Psych Services photograph.)

Park Place substation in the 1970s was home to the storied Park Place Rangers, known as HPD's toughest outfit where the strong always seem to survive. This archival photograph does not claim to depict the effectiveness of the Park Place Rangers. (HPD Archives.)

Sandy Byars, one of the few female HPD officers in uniform at the time, reports for duty on November 14, 1970. (HPD Archives.)

HPD liked to "celebrate" the receipt of new pieces of equipment. Here, Chief Herman B. Short tests the department's brand new microscope on October 11, 1972. (HPD Archives.)

The HPD Burglary and Theft Division poses on the steps of 61 Riesner Street in the 1990s. (HPD Archives.)

Chief Charles McClelland, appointed by Mayor Annise Parker in 2010, is pictured diligently at work at his desk, issuing orders and directions on an always-active computer. (Tom Kennedy.)

Someone from each division of the Houston Police Department is seen posed under the skyline of Space City in the 1990s. (HPD Archives.)

Six

PRESERVING AND PROTECTING

On his April 27, 1959, visit to
Houston, Cuban president Fidel
Castro was treated to some Texas
barbecue. Houston police officers
were with him to keep an eye
out for trouble. (*Houston Post*
photograph; courtesy of HMRC.)

Here is Fidel Castro literally surrounded by Houston police officers at a time before he was in tight with the USSR and posed a threat to the United States. (*Houston Post* photograph; courtesy of HMRC.)

This is an exceptionally historic HPD photograph taken November 21, 1963, the day before Pres. John F. Kennedy was assassinated in Dallas. Solo motorcycle officers were at Hobby Airport to escort JFK to downtown Houston. The HPD officers with President Kennedy are, from left to right, Pinky Wiggins, S.A. Cooper, Hugo Shine, E.J. Christian (shaking the President's hand), Bobby Foster, Lynn Maughmer, and Capt. Tom Sawyer. (Jim Kelley family.)

Taken by an unidentified photographer, here is another historic shot of President Kennedy the day before he was assassinated. The HPD officers are, from left to right, Lynn Maughmer, Dub Nickerson, Terrel Tissue, R.B. Sanford, Sgt. J.D. Black, and Roland English. (Jim Kelley family.)

Supreme Court Justice Thurgood Marshall (1908–1993) visited Houston in the late 1960s. At that time, there were no major hotels that would provide rooms to African Americans, so Justice Marshall was quartered in the home of Houston civil rights leader Judson Robinson Sr. Marshall (left) was guarded and driven to activities by HPD's Charles Howard, center, and Al Blair, right. Blair and Howard were longtime members of the HPD Criminal Intelligence Division. They were often assigned to protect visiting dignitaries. (Al Blair.)

Officer Al Blair provided local security for Pres. Ronald Reagan so often over the years that Reagan considered him a good friend. Here, at the airport after one of Reagan's arrivals, the president turned the tables on the officer when he acted like Blair was the center of attention instead of himself. (Al Blair.)

George H.W. Bush had just learned some great news the night of November 8, 1988. "They just told me I won the election," the newly elected president of the United States told the HPD solo motorcycle detail guarding his house in an exclusive west Houston neighborhood. The officers are, from left to right, Gary Blankinship, Glin Rudd, Sam Roccaforte, Tom Barnes, H.E. Prothro, J.E. Baker, unidentified, J.L. Kelley, Dale Boman, unidentified, B.W. Oliver, President Bush, R.H. Vahldiek, J.R. Boy, L.D. Lucky, unidentified, George Buehler, Jim Erby, unidentified in suit, unidentified woman, unidentified, and Lt. W.G. Eickenhorst. (Gary Blankinship.)

Senior Police Officer Gary Blankinship poses with First Lady Barbara Bush, a great friend of Houston police officers, outside the Bush home in Houston, where Blankinship and other solo motorcycle officers were assigned. (Gary Blankinship.)

Pres. Bill Clinton shakes the hand of the leader of his police escort team, Lt. W.G. Eickenhorst, who headed the solo motorcycle detail at the time. (W.G. Eickenhorst.)

Pictured on March 5, 1986, at Ellington Field in Houston are, from left to right, solo motorcycle officers T.D. Crawford, J.M. O'Brien, C.R. Black, J.H. Hill, Lt. W.G. Eickenhorst, R.D. Holtsscclaw, C.H. Brenham, Sgt. J.L. Fox, Vice Pres. George Bush and Barbara Bush, A.J. Mark, C.A. Contreras, H.A. Kelley, and S.A. Roccaforte. (W.G. Eickenhorst.)

Vice Pres. Richard Nixon visited Houston on a 1960 presidential campaign trip. Naturally, Houston's finest protected him. (*Houston Post* photograph by Owen Johnson; courtesy of HMRC.)

Hall of Fame home run king Hank Aaron of the Atlanta Braves is presented a Texas six-shooter during the 1974 season by two of Houston's finest, J.C. Wingo (left) and Julius Knigge. (Lance White.)

In his retirement, Gen. Douglas MacArthur came to Houston for a visit and graciously posed with this large group of Houston police officers, some of whom were Army veterans who served with him in World War II or the Korean War. (Pinky Wiggins family.)

Future police chief Harry Caldwell, left, and the current police chief Herman B. Short, right, are pictured in 1966 with actor James Whitmore, center. Chief Short was more famous for the picture he refused to have taken with actor John Wayne. "The Duke" had neglected to wear his toupee, and Short did not want to destroy the famed actor's movie persona. (HPD Archives.)

Daredevil showman Evel Knievil came to police headquarters on January 21, 1971, to pay his respects and have his picture taken. As one might expect, he went to the pressroom on the third floor of 61 Riesner Street down the hall from the police chief's office. It was there he met pressroom veterans, from left to right, Jack Weeks of the *Houston Chronicle*, Jack Cato of KPRC (Channel 2), and Bob Wolfe of KTRK (Channel 13). These three reporters probably covered more police stories than any other three reporters in Houston police history. (HPD Archives.)

Evel Knievil could not pay a visit to police headquarters without visiting the chief, Herman Short, right, who appears to be giving the daredevil some advice, as officer Sal Gambino looks on. (HPD Archives.)

Mounted patrol officers attract the attention of West German chancellor Helmut Kohl during his July 11, 1990, visit to Houston. (HPD Archives.)

Republican presidential candidate Robert Dole visited Houston on the campaign trail in 1996 and was met and escorted by this group of HPD officers. From left to right are Leroy "Bo" Weaver, Mike Navarro, J.J. Berry, Mr. Dole, Wayne Kirby, and Randall Johnson (J.J. Berry.)

As first lady, Nancy Reagan visited Houston and was greeted by HPD solo motorcycle officer J.J. Berry at the airport. To Berry's right are, in order, officers Rick Holtsclaw, James Lee, and Charlie Contreras. (J.J. Berry.)

Seven

PERSONALITIES

Lanny Dixon Stephenson (far right) was the first female homicide detective in American history. Stephenson began as a police matron at HPD in 1951 and became a policewoman two years later. In her 20 years, she once told an interviewer, "There was never a day I dreaded going to work. I always enjoyed going to work." One day, she married Woody Stephenson, the night police chief, on her lunch hour. After her police retirement, she served as a justice of the peace in Llano County, Texas. (HMRC.)

Elizabeth "Betsy" Watson was Houston's first-ever female police chief. A Kathy Whitmire appointee to succeed Lee P. Brown, Watson served two years, continuing Brown's Community-Oriented Policing. (HPD Archives.)

Officer Alvin Young joined HPD in the department's second cadet class in February 1949 and served 40 years. Young formed the African American Police Officers League in 1975 and was a nationally recognized marksman. By the early 1970s, he became the first black officer to teach marksmanship at the police academy. (May Walker.)

Officer May Walker became the department's first female solo patrol officer in 1975. After her HPD career, she was elected constable of Harris County Precinct Seven. (May Walker.)

HPD's pistol team competed in local, state, regional, and national pistol matches. They were regional champions at one point. Here, they are pictured displaying some of their trophies. The team included, from left to right, Lt. E.E. Milam, unidentified, Tommy Hrobar, unidentified, Bob Jennings, Virgil Wooley, M.D. Beale, J.D. Scrum (team captain), and Sgt. John Pohlman. (M.D. Beale.)

Officer Edward A. Thomas holds the record for the longest HPD tenure. He served from 1948 until his retirement in 2011, a period of 63 years. Everyone from the chief on down referred to him as "Mr. Thomas." (May Walker.)

In the 1990s, the department issued a set of police trading cards patterned after baseball cards. This card featured Chief Sam Nuchia, who served under Mayor Bob Lanier (1992–1998). (HPD Archives.)

Officer E.J. Stringfellow became the first African American city marshal in 1980. "String" later became the chief in the city marshal's office. (May Walker.)

The Houston Police Department named its Southeast Command Center after Marshal E.J. "String" Stringfellow. (Gary R. Hicks Sr.)

Sgt. Cynthia "Cindy" Jones Landry Massey is pictured at the top in the white hat. Clockwise from her are Maggie Marques, Regina Young, Phyliss Wunche, Lavonda Hobbs, and an unidentified officer. At that time, recruiting used this photograph for a hiring campaign targeted at women. For many years, the HPD administration refused to promote a woman to the rank of sergeant. Finally, in 1978, Police Chief Harry Caldwell promoted Cindy Massey to sergeant, making her the first ever female to hold the rank. The Massey name is well known in HPD history, beginning with Lt. Chester Massey. Massey's sons Richard and David joined HPD, as did Richard Junior and David's son Chris. Cindy married David Massey. (Cindy Massey.)

George Seber, left, was the only assistant HPD chief from the late 1940s until the mid-1960s. He is pictured here with Bernard Calkins, the chief operating officer of Houston Rapid Transit, the city's bus operators in the 1960s and 1970s. Seber came from several generations of Houston police officers. He held the second-highest rank in the department. (HPD Archives.)

Ephirne Leija became the first Hispanic captain in HPD history in 1980, a time when Chief Harry Caldwell was working diligently to improve HPD's relationship with Houston's Hispanics in the wake of a controversial and highly emotional death-in-custody case and some other negative incidents. Leija's promotion ceremony at police headquarters was the event of the year, drawing Hispanic schoolchildren from the new captain's neighborhood as well as his friends, neighbors, and church members. (HPD Archives.)

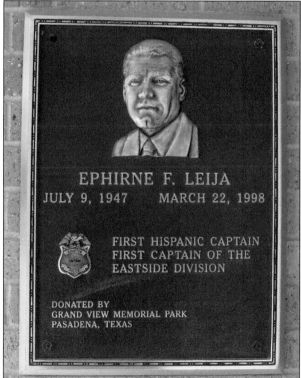

EPHIRNE F. LEIJA
JULY 9, 1947   MARCH 22, 1998

FIRST HISPANIC CAPTAIN
FIRST CAPTAIN OF THE
EASTSIDE DIVISION

DONATED BY
GRAND VIEW MEMORIAL PARK
PASADENA, TEXAS

Leija died of cancer in 1998 at age 51. The Leija Police Storefront on Galveston Road in the eastside patrol sector that Leija commanded was constructed and named in his memory. This plaque reminds all who enter of Leija and his work. (HPD Archives.)

In early 2002, HPD researchers found that Hispanics were victims of more than half the city's reported robberies, prompting robbery captain M.D. Brown to request Chief C.O. "Brad" Bradford to approve a temporary Latino Squad to address the growing policing problem. In its first year, the special Spanish-speaking squad compiled a 64-percent clearance rate, prompting Acting Police Chief Tim Oettmeier to make it a permanent HPD fixture. The original Latino squad included, from left to right, (first row) officer Eddie Rodriguez, officer Debbie Lahaie, Sgt. Michelle Ynosencio, officer Art Mejia, Sgt. Daniel Silva, and Executive Assistant Chief Tim Oettmeier; (second row) Lt. H. Lopez, Sgt. Steve Guerra, officer Richard Rodriguez, Sgt. Joel Rodriguez, Sgt. Roger Chappell, officer P. Reese, officer Darryl Cherry, and officer Ciro Martinez. (Tim Oettmeier.)

Nobody in Houston history had a more distinctive style than Marvin Zindler. A native Houstonian from a family in retailing, Marvin loved law enforcement and show business. In the war years, he served as one of a few hundred auxiliary police officers, who were not academy-trained but carried sidearms and helped the real officers. Zindler is pictured here in his auxiliary police officer's uniform, posing with his trusty pistol, which he actually fired one night when he and Red Smith, a real HPD officer, spotted a burglar in Marvin's family clothing store. Alas, Marvin surrendered his badge for violating auxiliary police policy. (HMRC.)

Here, from the HPD Museum, is an auxiliary police badge like the one once worn by Marvin Zindler. (HPD Museum.)

Whereas the less prurient *Houston Post* and *Houston Chronicle* shied away from blood in their pictures, the *Houston Press* went in the opposite direction, as evidenced by this Marvin Zindler picture of a nighttime crime victim. (Zindler family.)

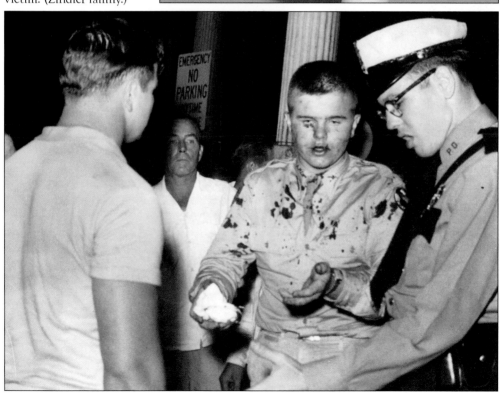

In the 1960s and early 1970s, Houston officers, particularly homicide detectives, drafted news reporters to fill out their lineups. This photograph features Jack Cato, far right, generally conceded to be the best police reporter in Houston news media history. Cato is the only "suspect" who has not been blurred from identification. He gained fame for getting Elmer Wayne Henley to confess to killing "the Candy Man," Dean Corll, to Corll's mother on Cato's car phone. Such devices were unique in 1973 and much more complicated than today's cell phones. Henley was one of Corll's two accomplices who helped abduct, rape, torture, and murder a minimum of 28 boys from 1970 to 1973. The crimes came to light only after Henley shot and killed Corll and told his mother about it as the camera rolled. (Harris County Archives.)

At six feet, eight inches, and weighing more than 300 pounds, Tiny Romund was the biggest Houston police officer of his era, which was primarily the 1950s. Tiny's patrol car had special suspension to accommodate a driver as heavy as he was. Despite his intimidating size, Officer Romund was a gentle giant whose career thrived on helping kids stay out of trouble. Tiny was often described as an ambassador to Houston who represented the HPD at various school functions, portraying a positive image. (HPPU Archives.)

One or two or three Zoch brothers served the HPD from 1954 thought 2004. Together, the three brothers put in 96 years of service. They are, from left to right, Lt. Nelson Zoch, 36 years, retired as a homicide lieutenant in 2004; Lt. Herman A. "John" Zoch, 27 years, retired from the Robbery Division in 1983; and Capt. Leroy N. Zoch, 33 years, retired as the captain in charge of the Robbery Division in 1987. (Nelson Zoch.)

For the first and only time in Houston history, the mayor dipped down to the sergeant ranks to pick his chief. On September 1, 1954, Mayor Roy Hofheinz chose Sgt. Jack Heard to lead the HPD. At 36, Heard was the same age as his father, Percy Heard, when the elder member of the family became chief on August 1, 1930. Jack Heard served two years before accepting a high-ranking position with the Texas Department of Corrections. He later became sheriff of Harris County. (Jack Heard family.)

Police Chief C.O. "Brad" Bradford served as Houston's police chief from 1996 until 2003, under both Mayor Bob Lanier and Mayor Lee Brown, the first African American police chief of Houston. Bradford was the second African American to serve as chief, and Chief Harold Hurtt (2004–2009) was the third. Charles McClelland, the chief in 2012, was the fourth. In 2011, Bradford was serving his second two-year term as an at-large member of the Houston City Council. (HPD Archives.)

In 2012, Martha Montalvo was serving as the HPD's first-ever Hispanic female executive assistant police chief. (HPD Archives.)

HPD's Narcotics Canine Detail team posed for this group picture in Minute Maid Park, taken June 26, 2005. (HPD Archives.)

Lois Gibson is recorded in *The Guinness Book of World Records* as "The World's Most Successful Forensic Artist." Her sketches have helped law enforcement bring in over 1,062 criminals. That number grows every day at HPD. (Tom Kennedy.)

Solo motorcycle officer Jim Kelley was a legend around the HPD. He had a four-digit badge number in his early years, and quit the department for a while but later returned. When he got his new badge, he realized that HPD badge No. 1 was available. He wore it, made it famous, and passed it to his son Don when he followed in his daddy's footsteps to the HPD. Jim Kelley "rode point," meaning he led solo motorcycle details when they escorted dignitaries, rock stars, and other famous people. Kelley rode point for Pres. John F. Kennedy's limousine on November 21, 1963, in Houston, one day before he was assassinated in Dallas. Upon retiring after 25 years, "Jimmy" opened a chain of Kelley's Country Cookin' restaurants, favorites of Houstonians and surrounding suburban towns. Kelley died in 2009 at age 71. (Jim Kelley family.)

This badge No. 1 in the HPD Museum resembled the one Kelley and his son Donnie wore in their HPD careers, a contradiction to the common belief that an officer from the early 1900s would wear such an early badge number. (HPD Museum.)

Mayor Fred Hofheinz pins the sergeant's badge on J.C. Hartman, the first African American HPD police sergeant in 1974. (J.C. Hartman.)

J.C. Hartman, the first-ever African American HPD sergeant, was previously a professional baseball player. Hartman played in the storied negro leagues of the 1950s before taking the field at shortstop for the minor-league Houston Buffs and, in 1962 and 1963, for the Houston Colt .45s of the National League. (Bill Dorrill.)

The number of HPD members of the Law Enforcement Association for Asian Pacifics (LEAAP) continues to grow in 2012. Pictured here are the HPD officers who attended the 1998 Asian Officers' San Francisco Conference. They are, from left to right, officer Steven Kang, officer Connie Park, officer Edwin Lem, Sgt. Lily Yep, officer Michael Wong, and officer Tom Nguyen. (Ed Lem.)

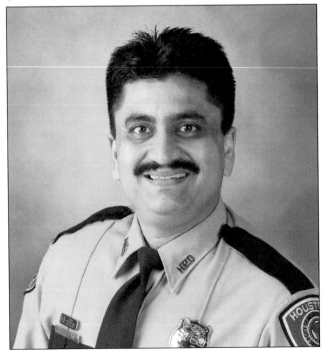

HPD officer Muzaffar Siddiqi became the department's liaison to Houstonians from Middle Eastern and South Asian countries in 2000. HPD became the only police department in the nation with crime prevention handbooks published in 15 different languages. In 2012, there were more than 250,000 Houston residents from India, Iran, Turkey, Pakistan, Saudi Arabia, Sri Lanka, Bangladesh, and Qatar. (HPD photograph.)

Eight

MEETING AND CONFERRING

This picture, taken in 1947, is one of the most significant in the history of the Houston Police Department. Texas governor Buford Jester (seated) is signing into law a measure that provided state civil service protection for Houston police officers. Prior to this bill becoming law, the mayor of Houston appointed and fired any officer at will. Frequently, an officer's job was dependent on which candidate he hung signs for on Election Day. The primary backer of the effort was the Houston Police Officers Association, formed in 1945. The association had many strong leaders, especially Breck Porter, standing over Jester's left shoulder. Other HPOA leaders present for the historic signing were, from left to right, T.C. Christian, John Irwin, and (at the far right) Red Squyers. (HPOU Archives.)

Hans Marticiuc began 12 years of service as the first president of the newly formed Houston Police Officers Union in 1995. The newly constituted union included members of both the Houston Police Officers Association and the Houston Police Patrolmen's Union (HPPU) and offered member officers unprecedented insurance and legal benefits. HPOU, under Marticiuc and executive director Mark Clark, were successful in getting new state meet-and-confer rights needed for the union to negotiate five-year contracts with the city for the first time in history. Marticiuc is known as the father of meet and confer, which remains the greatest benefit enhancer in Houston police history. He retired from the HPD in 2011. (HPOU Archives.)

One-time association/union president Mark Clark later became executive director of the Houston Police Officers Union. Clark was a determined advocate of political action committees (PACs) to screen candidates and make contributions to specified campaigns. His leadership firmly established HPOU in the meet-and-confer process that solidified police benefits through a contractual arrangement with the City of Houston. Presidential candidates, such as Bill Clinton, always eagerly seek the nod from HPOU. (HPOU Archives.)

Republican presidential candidate George W. Bush, who was governor of Texas at the time, sought out the political advice of HPOU executive director Mark Clark as one of the state's longtime leaders in the politics of policing and police benefits. (HPOU Archives.)

Bob Thomas was the leader of the founders of the Houston Police Patrolmen's Union (HPPU) on October 22, 1979. HPPU advocated better legal representation and insurance benefits than the rival Houston Police Officers Association. Making good on these promises, among others, the HPPU soon rivaled the HPOA in membership numbers. But both groups realized in 1995 that a meet-and-confer law from the legislature was nearly impossible to get passed without one union representing the majority of HPD officers. (Bob Thomas.)

The HPPU founders, from right to left, were Chris Gillespie, Ramon McFarland, Bob Thomas, Tommy Britt, Doug Carr, and Rick Ashwood. Thomas was the founding president and chief spokesman. The new union used aggressive press conferences and public stances to emphasize the city's mistreatment of officers on the street. Indeed, the majority of HPPU members were officers and sergeants, while the HPOA leadership was top-heavy with captains and lieutenants. Most HPPU members joined the newly formed HPOU in 1995, setting the state for meet and confer. (HPPU Archives.)

This is a copy of the newspaper ad and poster paid for by friends of officer Tim Hearn and fellow Waltrip High School alumni who became Houston police officers. Hearn, University of Texas accounting graduate, became president of Houston Police Academy class No. 67. He had been a Houston officer four years when a lifelong criminal, who later got the death penalty, shot him to death on the night of June 8, 1978. Hearn was a very popular officer, as evidenced by the number of fellow officers, active and retired, from Waltrip High. The ad has been placed in the *Leader* newspaper every year to mark the anniversary of his death. (Bob Thomas.)

Retired homicide lieutenant Nelson Zoch worked with the HPOU and the 100 Club of Greater Houston to establish the practice of placing special line-of-duty death markers at the final resting sites of each Houston police officer who made the ultimate sacrifice. Here, Zoch places a marker at the gravesite of officer George Edwards, who was shot to death in June 1939 in a struggle with an auto theft suspect. (Tom Kennedy.)

HPOU leader Gary Blankinship (left), a longtime solo motorcycle officer, poses here with Clem Jankowski (center) and Houston mayor Bob Lanier (1992–1998). Blankinship was later HPOU president. (HPOU Archives.)

Texas governor Preston Smith signs a new state civil service law that further establishes the benefits of Houston police officers. With the governor, from left to right, are Houston Police Officers Association leader Julius Knigge, state senator Chet Brooks, association president A.J. Burke, W.G. Eickenhorst, unidentified, and R.C. Rich. (HPOU Archives.)

The Houston Police Officers Union strongly endorses the Blue Santa program, in which officers contribute money throughout the year to buy presents for needy families with young children at Christmas. Each year, Blue Santa serves 12,000 to 15,000 needy kids. Senior Police Officer Freddie Joe Pyland is a primary leader in the program; the program's spokesman is Houston Texans' star wide receiver Andre Johnson. Pyland is depicted on the card with Blue Santa, aka officer David Mireles. (F.J. Pyland.)

Each year during Police Week in May, the HPOU takes the lead in honoring the memory of each and every officer who died in the line of duty. Here, officers line the granite memorial, the creation of Jesus Bautista Moroles in 1990, during the 2010 ceremony. The Houston Police Memorial is aptly located on Memorial Drive in the shadows of the downtown skyline and a literal stone's throw from the HPOU Building on State Street. The crowd always gathers for the event at the Union Building and walks or rides the short distance to the memorial. (Mary Pyland.)

Earl Maughmer, who retired as an HPD captain, was an early leader in the fight to get civil service protection for Houston police officers. Prior to the efforts of brave officers like Maughmer, Breck Porter, and others, officers could keep their jobs based on which mayoral candidate they supported. If their candidate lost, the officers were usually fired or demoted. (HPD Archives.)

Jim Kilty was a popular Houston police officer and member of the Houston Police Officers Association (later known as the HPOU). In the 1970s, Kilty, as a patrol officer in the drug culture/hippie community known as Montrose, promoted a pigs-versus-hippies softball game that proved to be a successful bonding experience. Kilty joined the narcotics division and, sadly, was shot and killed during the arrest of a drug suspect on April 8, 1976. (HPOU Archives.)

"The badge means you care" was a bumper sticker the department used in the late 1970s for recruiting purposes. The badge depicted on the sticker was No. 1856, the badge worn by officer Jim Kilty. (Mark Kilty.)

Louis Kuba, a Houston police officer only 34 days out of the academy, was one of many officers assigned to what became a brief riot that erupted on the campus of Texas Southern University on May 17, 1967, after nearly two months of racial unrest, fostered primarily by outside influences. HPD officers sealed off the campus when sniper fire from dormitories held about 200 officers at bay for 40 minutes. Officer Kuba was struck in the head by a high-caliber slug and was pronounced dead a short time later. Houston held the distinction of having the only riot in which more whites were killed than African Americans. The only person killed was Officer Kuba. His gravesite is specially marked in Houston's Forest Park Lawndale Cemetery. (Nelson Zoch.)

The police union is not responsible for the HPD Burial Fund. But this special fund was set up by the same type of strident leadership that formed the Houston Police Officers Association right after World War II. Before 1921, Houston officers had no burial benefits or pension. The burial fund started with $181.50 but soon grew with the proceeds of special events. The first one was the Policeman's Ball and Jazz Review on March 17, 1921. It consisted of skits and music by officers and included six officers' wives playing banjos. Over the years, the fundraising event grew to be more sophisticated, as this 1947 advertisement attests. (Thompson's Antique Center of Texas.)

117

The Houston Gunners football team plays in the National Public Safety Football League and won the National Championship in 1999. The team consists primarily of HPD officers but also includes sheriff's deputies and deputy constables. HPOU is one of the team sponsors, offering funding for stadium rental and referee salaries. (Sgt. Robert Bell.)

Not only was Breck Porter, second from left, a leader in the crusade to get civil service protection for Houston police officers, he also took the lead to recognize every HPD officer who died in the line of duty. Recognition of these great fallen heroes remains a primary objective of the Houston Police Officers Union, the new name given the association in 1995 when it became a nationally affiliated union. With Porter in this in 1948 picture are officer B.M. "Red" Squyres on the left and Chief B.W. Payne on the right. (HPOU Archives.)

The 100 Club presented a special plaque and survivor benefits to Sherry Riley and daughter, Shane O'Dell Riley, the survivors of officer Jerry Lawrence Riley, who was killed in the line of duty on June 18, 1974, when his patrol car was struck by a tractor-trailer rig when he and his partner were responding to assist an officer. Both the 100 Club and the union (known as the association in 1974) provide assistance to the surviving wives or husbands of Houston officers killed in the line of duty. Pictured with Sherry Riley are HPOA president A.J. Burke on the left, the 100 Club president in the center, and Chief Carrol Lynn on the right. The check was presented on August 3, 1974. (HPD Archives.)

The Houston Police Officers Union honored Lt. Breckenridge Porter for his service aimed at improving the benefits of all Houston officers by naming the union structure on State Street the Breckenridge Porter Building. The Porter Building is now part of a growing HPOU complex that includes the four-story structure on the right. HPOU represents all but about 165 of HPD's force of 5,400 officers, making it one of the strongest police unions in the nation. (Tom Kennedy.)

In the 1960s, Houston's biggest rodeo event was known as the Fat Stock Show and Rodeo, while today it is the Houston Livestock Show and Rodeo. Movie and television stars Roy Rogers and Dale Evans provided the entertainment at one of the 1960s shows. They are pictured here with, from left to right, Officer Gleghorn, an unidentified Fat Stock Show honoree, and Sgts. Kirby and Easter. (HPOU Archives.)

On January 25, 2012, Mayor Annise Parker swore in the Houston Police Officers Union board members. Pictured are, from left to right, J.G. Garza, Tim Butler, Terry Wolfe, Terry Seagler, Police Chief Charles McClelland, Robert Breiding, Jon Yencha, Dana Hitzman, Mayor Parker, Steve Turner, Bubba Caldwell (hidden), Tom Hayes, Paul Ogden, HPOU president Ray Hunt, Will Reiser, First Vice President Doug Griffith, Jeff Wagner, Luis Menendez, Marsha Todd, George Shaw, Joslyn Johnson, Bill Booth, Lance Gibson, O.J. Latin, Secretary Joe Castaneda, Michael Navarro, and Joseph Gamaldi. (Mary Pyland.)

Nine

SERVING WITH HONOR

The Houston Police Foundation, founded on the watch of Police Chief Harold Hurtt (2004–2009), connects private investment dollars with effective public safety solutions, leveraging private resources to fund high-priority HPD needs. In this photograph, Chief Hurtt, third from the right, is flanked by, from left to right, foundation executive director Charlene Floyd and foundation board members Paul Somerville, Rey Gonzales, Tilman Fertitta, Dave Ward, and Bill Nelson. Fertitta serves as chairman. Ward, the longtime KTRK-TV (Channel 13) anchorman, serves as emcee at the annual Police Week Awards at Fertitta's Downtown Acquarian restaurant. (Houston Police Foundation.)

The HPD Honor Guard participates in every Police Week ceremony as well as at the memorial services of all current and retired officers. (Mary Pyland.)

Police chief Jack Heard set up the HPD chaplain service in 1955, but it did not firmly take hold until 1977, when Bubba Hanna, far right, was named HPD chaplain. Serving until 1984, Hanna was succeeded by Floyd Lewis, to Hanna's right, in 1988 and Edwin Davis from 1992 until 2005. Current HPD chaplain Monty Montgomery, far left, began his service in 2006. The chaplain presides at all memorial services during Police Week as well as at funerals of current and retired police officers. (Monty Montgomery.)

Senior Police Officer David Freytag, known as the "Father of the Honor Guard," presents a memorial wreath to Mayor Bill White and Chief Harold Hurtt during Police Week ceremonies at the Houston Police Memorial around 2006. (Mary Pyland.)

The honor guard's David Freytag presents the American flag to the widow and family of officer Henry Canales at Canales's memorial ceremony. Officer Canales was shot and killed while conducting an undercover investigation into the sale of stolen televisions on June 23, 2009. (Mary Pyland.)

Liv Abernethy, daughter of slain Houston officer Tim Abernethy, clutches a flag presented to the family at Abernethy's memorial service. The officer's wife, Stephanie, and son T.J. are seated next to Liv. Officer Abernethy was shot and killed during a foot pursuit of a suspect who fled following a traffic stop on December 7, 2008. His killer received the Texas death penalty. (Mary Pyland.)

Retired homicide lieutenant Nelson Zoch has ardently researched every line-of-duty death in HPD history from 1841 to the present. In 2006, he authored *Fallen Heroes of the Bayou City*. The first edition was a sellout. The book contains many details about the crimes as well as the fates of the perpetrators. (Nelson Zoch.)

The memorial service of officer Rodney Johnson in 2006 was one of the most dramatic of its kind. Johnson's funeral saw thousands of Houstonians lining the streets and freeways in the miles-long trip from the church to the cemetery. Officer Johnson was shot seven times and killed after taking an illegal alien into custody during a traffic stop on September 21, 2006. His widow also was an HPD officer, Sgt. Joslyn Johnson. (Mary Pyland.)

In 2012, Rick Hartley was serving as the executive director of the 100 Club of Greater Houston. The group was founded in 1953 with the mission of providing line-of duty death benefits to the surviving families of the officers. In May 2006, the club began providing benefits statewide to dependants of commissioned personnel with the Texas Department of Public Safety, Texas Parks and Wildlife Department, and Texas Alcohol and Beverage Commission, and institutional personnel with the Texas Department of Criminal Justice. In this picture, Hartley demonstrates the club's commitment to the special gravesite markers for HPD's fallen heroes. (Tom Kennedy.)

Fallen Heroes
of the Houston
Police Department

March 10, 1860 – C. Edward Foley
March 17, 1883 – Richard Snow
February 8, 1886 – Henry Williams
March 15, 1891 – James E. Fenn
July 30, 1901 – William F. Weiss
December 11, 1901 – Herman Youngst
December 11, 1901 – John C. James
April 1, 1910 – William E. Murphy
August 4, 1911 – John M. Cain
October 18, 1912 – Joseph Robert Free
May 24, 1914 – Isaac "Ike" Parsons
August 23, 1917 – Rufus H. Daniels
August 23, 1917 – E.G. Meinke
August 23, 1917 – Horace Moody
August 23, 1917 – Ross Patton
August 23, 1917 – Ira D. Raney
February 19, 1921 – Johnnie Davidson
June 19, 1921 – Jeter Young
June 27, 1921 – Davie Murdock
August 23, 1924 – J. Clark Etheridge
January 21, 1925 – Pete Corrales
September 17, 1925 – E.C. Chavez
January 30, 1927 – Perry Page Jones
July 30, 1927 – R.Q. Wells
March 14, 1928 – Carl Greene
April 22, 1928 – Paul W. Whitlock
June 17, 1928 – Albert Worth Davis
June 22, 1929 – Oscar Hope
September 13, 1929 – Ed Jones
December 17, 1929 – C.F. Thomas
September 30, 1930 – Edward D. Fitzgerald
September 30, 1930 – W.B. Pharres
December 3, 1930 – J.D. Landry
October 16, 1933 – Harry Mereness
March 9, 1935 – R.H. "Rimps" Sullivan
December 1, 1936 – James T. "Jim" Gambill
November 8, 1937 – Adolph P. Martial

March 24, 1938 – Marion E. Palmer
June 30, 1939 – George Edwards
August 18, 1946 – H.B. Hammond
January 12, 1954 – S.A. "Buster" Kent
February 24, 1954 – Fred Maddox Jr.
April 30, 1955 – Jack B. Beets
April 30, 1955 – Charles R. Gougenheim
November 30, 1955 – Frank L. Kellogg
August 24, 1956 – Robert Schultea
June 5, 1958 – Noel R. Miller
March 20, 1959 – Claude E. Branon
August 23, 1959 – John W. Suttle
February 28, 1960 – Gonsalo Q. Gonzales
March 8, 1963 – James T. Walker
August 4, 1963 – Charles R. McDaniel
July 1, 1964 – James F. Willis
February 18, 1965 – Herbert N. Planer
June 30, 1965 – Floyd T. Deloach Jr.
January 21, 1967 – Louis L. Sander
May 17, 1967 – Louis R. Kuba
June 26, 1968 – Ben E. Gerhart
June 26, 1968 – Bobby L. James
November 26, 1969 – Kenneth W. Moody
January 31, 1970 – Leon Griggs
January 31, 1971 – Robert W. Lee
December 10, 1971 – Claude R. Beck
June 17, 1972 – David E. Noel
October 26, 1972 – Jerry Leon Spruill
January 9, 1973 – Antonio Guzman Jr.
September 19, 1973 – David Huerta
June 18, 1974 – Jerry L. Riley
January 30, 1975 – Johnny T. Bamsch
August 2, 1975 – F.E. Wright
October 10, 1975 – R.H. Calhoun
January 28, 1976 – George G. Rojas
April 8, 1976 – James F. Kilty
June 8, 1978 – Timothy L. Hearn

August 16, 1979 – Charles Baker
October 2, 1980 – Victor R. Wells III
April 18, 1981 – Jose A. Zamarron
March 29, 1982 – Winston J. Rawlins
March 29, 1982 – William E. DeLeon
April 28, 1982 – Daryl W. Shirley
July 13, 1982 – James D. Harris
August 18, 1982 – Kathleen Schaefer
February 23, 1983 – Charles R. Coates
September 12, 1983 – William Moss
April 10, 1987 – Maria M. Groves
February 18, 1988 – Andrew Winzer
July 19, 1988 – Elston Howard
November 10, 1989 – Florentino M. Garcia Jr.
December 9, 1989 – James C. "Boz" Boswell
June 27, 1990 – James B. Irby
November 25, 1990 – John A. Salvaggio
April 12, 1991 – Bruno D. Soboleski
January 6, 1994 – Michael P. Roman

January 31, 1994 – Guy P. Gaddis
November 12, 1994 – David M. Healy
December 24, 1995 – Dawn S. Erickson
April 6, 1997 – Cuong H. "Tony" Trinh
May 23, 1998 – Kent D. Kincaid
May 19, 1999 – Troy A. Blando
September 20, 2000 – Jerry K. Stowe
January 10, 2001 – Dennis E. Holmes
May 22, 2001 – Alberto Vasquez
March 7, 2002 – Keith A. Dees
April 3, 2003 – Charles R. Clark
March 25, 2004 – Frank M. Cantu Jr.
October 26, 2005 – Rueben B. Deleon
September 21, 2006 – Rodney Johnson
June 29, 2008 – Gary Allen Gryder
December 7, 2008 – Timothy Abernethy
June 23, 2009 – Henry Canales
May 19, 2010 – Eydelmen Mani
May 29, 2011 – Kevin Will

At the October 2010 general membership meeting of the Houston Police Officers Union, Alisha Will and her newborn son, Kevin Will Jr., were in attendance to receive HPOU line-of-duty death benefits. HPOU president Gary Blankinship made the presentation along with HPOU's Krystal LaReau. Officer Will died May 29, 2011, at the hands of a DWI suspect on the North Loop freeway. The union does a special dues assessment to help surviving families in line-of-duty deaths. These come in addition to 100 Club benefits. (Mary Pyland.)

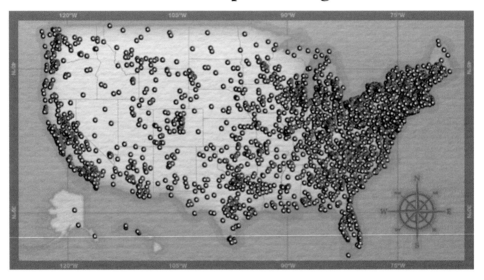